THE
BIRKENHEAD
DRILL

THE
BIRKENHEAD
DRILL

Their choice it was plain between drownin' in 'eaps
an' bein' mopped by the screw,
So they stood an' was still to the Birken'ead *Drill,*
soldier an' sailor too!

—KIPLING

By Douglas W. Phillips

PUBLISHED IN THE YEAR OF THE 150TH ANNIVERSARY
OF THE GREAT ACT OF BRAVERY

THE VISION FORUM, INC.
SAN ANTONIO, TEXAS

DEDICATION

On September 11, 2001, feminism died in the basement of the Word Trade Center. For the first time in a generation, the American people were exposed to the images and sounds of bold manhood sacrificing for women and children, as more than three hundred firefighters, all of them men, gave their lives in a burning inferno. That same day, three fathers aboard a hijacked jet decided to rush a band of Christ-hating zealots rather than allow their plane to be a tool in the hands of the Islamic enemies of our nation. In so doing, these fathers probably saved a national landmark and the lives of untold thousands. May the memory of these men serve to inspire young boys of future generations to raise the standard of Christian chivalry in a world that often forgets that God made men the protectors and defenders of women and children.

CONTENTS

The Loss of the Birkenhead

Right on our flank the crimson sun went down,
    The deep sea rolled around in dark repose,
When, like the wild shriek from some captured town,
A cry of women rose.

The stout ship *Birkenhead* lay hard and fast,
    Caught, without hope, upon a hidden rock;
Her timbers thrilled as nerves, when through them passed
The spirit of that shock.

And ever like base cowards, who leave their ranks
    In danger's hour, before the rush of steel,
Drifted away, disorderly, the planks
From underneath her keel.

Confusion spread, for, though the coast seemed near,
    Sharks hovered thick along that white sea-brink.
The boats could hold?—not all; and it was clear
She was about to sink.

"Out with those boats, and let us haste away,"
    Cried one, "ere yet yon sea the bark devours."
The man thus clamoring was, I scarce need say,
No officer of ours.

We knew our duty better than to care
    For such loose babblers, and made no reply,
Till our good colonel gave the word, and there
Formed us in line to die.

There rose no murmur from the ranks, no thought,
    By shameful strength, unhonored life to seek;
Our post to quit we were not trained, nor taught
To trample down the weak.

So we made women with their children go,
    The oars ply back again, and yet again;
Whilst, inch by inch, the drowning ship sank low,
Still under steadfast men.

What follows, why recall? The brave who died,
    Died without flinching in the bloody surf;
They sleep as well, beneath that purple tide,
As others, under turf;—

They sleep as well, and, roused from their wild grave,
    Wearing their wounds like stars, shall rise again,
Joint-heirs with Christ, because they bled to save
His weak ones, not in vain.

If that day's work no clasp or medal mark,
    If each proud heart no cross of bronze may press,
Nor cannon thunder loud from Tower and Park,
This feel we, none the less:

That those whom God's high grace there saved from ill—
Those also, left His martyrs in the bay—
Though not by siege, though not in battle, still
Full well had earned their pay.

Sir Francis Hastings Doyle

Chapter 1
MULTI-GENERATIONAL MANHOOD

The same thing that entered into the training of these men, knights, pioneers ... must enter into the training of the boy scouts of today. Just as they respected women and served them, so the tenderfoot and the scout must be polite and kind to women, not merely to well-dressed women, but to poorly dressed women; not merely to young women, but to old women: to women wherever they may be found—wherever they may be. To these a scout must always be courteous and helpful. When a scout is walking with a lady or a child, he should always walk on the outside of the sidewalk, so that he can better protect them against the jostling crowds. This rule is only altered when crossing the street, when the scout should get between

the lady and the traffic, so as to shield her from
accident or mud. Also in meeting a woman or child, a
scout, as matter of course, should always make way for
them even if he himself has to step off the sidewalk
into the mud. When riding in a street car or train a
scout should never allow a woman, an elderly person,
or a child to stand, but will offer his seat; and when he
does it he should do it cheerfully and with a smile.

—*Boy Scout Handbook*
1911 pg. 243-244

One year before the sinking of the R.M.S. *Titanic*, Lord
Baton-Powell, the visionary founder of Boy Scouting
worldwide, penned the above words for his very first
Boy Scout Handbook. His mission was to communicate the
practical outworking of Christian chivalry to the next
generation of boys. It should be remembered that the idea that
men were to act and live deferentially on behalf of women and
children, though an ancient principle, was already under attack
by 1911 from militant suffragettes intent on leveling the
political playing field by removing from the public mindset the
notion that women were a "weaker sex" in need of saving.

In calling for the boys of the twentieth century to live by
the historic code of masculine sacrifice, Baton-Powell was
adding his own part to a legacy of bold manhood which for
generations had not only constituted the warp and woof of
Christendom's patriarchal ethic, but which Baton-Powell and
some of his contemporaries had personally experienced during
the grueling South African campaigns of the nineteenth
century.[1] From the siege of Mafeking to the Battle of Rork's
Drift, young men and old serving Queen and country in South

Africa were called upon to live by this vision of manhood, often at great personal expense.

Heroism does not emerge from a vacuum. It is cultivated multi-generationally. It is nurtured through proverb and living example. It is impressed upon the minds and hearts of the young through the retelling of stories. And so it was that the very chivalric ethic which Baton-Powell would one day seek to advance through Scouting, was part of the heritage of his youth and the legacy of a group of South Africa-bound soldiers who laid the foundation for a maritime principle of "women and children first." A principle that would one day be repeated during the most famous nautical disaster in history.

Sixty years before those sacred words were uttered by the captain of the R.M.S. *Titanic*, a similar order was given, and this time in the face of near certain death to drowning or shark attack. That story, the subject of this book, would inspire generations of men to do their part in times of crisis and would one day be immortalized by the pen of Rudyard Kipling as "Soldier and Sailor Too."

---

1 During the Boer War, Robert Baton-Powell was assigned to protect the Mafeking province of South Africa. Baton-Powell and the 1,000 men with whom he served successfully defended themselves from a siege army of 9,000 Boers. The fighting was brutal and protracted. The exhausted British troops needed help. Baton-Powell demonstrated creativity and coolness under fire by recruiting and training boys 11 to 15 years of age who were too young to serve as soldiers, but who could relieve the regular troops of special duties. These boys, dubbed the Mafeking Cadet Corps, took responsibility for serving as runners, signalers, messengers, and first aid attendants. The siege lasted 217 days, but the British came out victorious, the little boys of the Cadet Corps gained world renown, and Baton-Powell became a British national hero.

Chapter 2
THE STORY OF THE BIRKENHEAD

The facts surrounding the sinking of the *Birkenhead* story are as follows. On January 8, 1852, the H.M. Troopship *Birkenhead* set sail on a transport mission for Algoa Bay off the coast of South Africa. Aboard were approximately 640 men, women, and children, including a large contingent of British troops bound for the Kaffir wars. At 2:00 a.m. in the morning of February 26, she struck a ledge off Cape Danger. Refusing to break ranks, the men stood at attention while the women and children disembarked on lifeboats. An order was given to stay clear of these small boats to prevent capsizing them and risking the loss of a woman or child. Twenty minutes after *Birkenhead* had hit the rock, she was submerged. Within a matter of hours, the majority of the men who had been aboard were either drowned or consumed by man-eating sharks.

Every woman and child lived.

History, of course, is more than the recitation of mere facts. It is the formal remembrance and the meaningful retelling of human passions and choices in motion. It is the interpretation of those facts such that we can understand and learn from the many providences of God in human events.

This is why the story of the *Birkenhead* remains relevant one hundred and fifty years after its sinking. A boat sank. So what? Behind the simple facts of the *Birkenhead* lies the answer to the heart and soul of Christendom. Namely, that to be great our civilization must rest on the transcendent truths demonstrated through the life, death, and resurrection of Jesus Christ.

Here is the story of men who maintained discipline, followed orders, and set the standard for generations to come of chivalrous conduct during a maritime disaster. The men would not only give up their seats on lifeboats for women and children, but would agree to forgo any attempt to swim for the overcrowded boats, rather than risk the lives of the women and children.

And so, rather than remembering an unfortunate disaster, we find in the *Birkenhead* the story of the mercy of God communicated through the principle that the strong die for the weak. "Greater love hath no man than this, that a man lay down his life for his friends" (John 15:13). Just as Jesus died for His bride, so too men are to die for theirs.

The Beginnings of the Birkenhead

At the time of her launch, the *Birkenhead* was the crowning glory of her generation of ships. The first iron-hulled vessel of war, she would prove to be unusually fast compared to other paddleboats. Before the *Birkenhead* set sail for her final journey, her unique design and excellent speed had earned hers the respect of the British Admiralty. She certainly was regarded with favor when it was discovered that she could accomplish in 45 days the same journey to the Cape of Good Hope that would take other vessels 64 days. Also contributing to her fame was the fact that in August of 1847, she managed under very difficult circumstances to free and tow to safety the S.S. *Great Britain*, which had been inadvertently beached.

Although the initial concept for the *Birkenhead* was to build her as a wooden-hulled frigate, plans for her purpose and construction later changed and it was agreed that she would serve as a troopship.

Dubbed the H.M. Paddle Steamer *Birkenhead*, she was designed by John Laird, built by the shipyard of Laird's of Birkenhead, and launched by the Marchioness of Westminster. At 210 feet in length, a displacement of 1,900 tons, and engines capable of 350 horsepower, she was a formidable vessel for her day.

The Final Voyage

The final journey of the *Birkenhead* began on January 7, 1852, as she set sail from Ireland for Africa under the command of Captain Robert Salmond of the Royal Navy. Her mission was routine: Deliver reinforcement troops and their wives and families to the Cape of Good Hope. The troops, including drafts from the 43rd Light Infantry, the 12th Lancers, and the 2nd, 6th, 12th, 45th, 73rd, 74th, and 91st Foot were to join Sir Harry Smith, the Governor for the Cape, to reinforce British efforts in the Kaffir War. Unknown to the passengers and troops aboard that day was the fact that Governor Smith was expecting more than just military reinforcements. Hidden deep within the hold of the *Birkenhead* was a treasure trove of gold to be delivered to him as part of a military pay packet.

The troops on *Birkenhead* were under the direct command of a sturdy 38-year-old British officer named Lieutenant-Colonel Alexander Seton of the 74th Highlanders. The precise number of passengers is still in dispute, but it is believed that there were approximately 640 individuals aboard.

For the most part, the journey was uneventful. The troopship made stops at Madeira, Sierra Leone, St. Helena, and finally docked in Simons Bay on February 23 where she took on fresh supplies before leaving on Wednesday the 25th for the Cape.

The Disaster

She was traveling at a smooth 8.5 knots when the *Birkenhead* found herself off course and perilously close to the aptly named Cape Danger. Mariners had long recognized the perils of the Cape, and precautions had been taken by Captain Salmond for rounding the cape. Nevertheless, something went sorely amiss.

Sometime just before 2:00 a.m. on the morning of February 26, 1852, the *Birkenhead* struck a rock ledge that would cause her to founder less than one mile from the beach of Danger Point.

At the moment of impact, the rock tore mercilessly through the metal hull. The damage was immediate and irreversible. For the men sleeping in bunks below the aft in the lower decks, there would be no opportunity for survival. Cold water immediately surged into their hold drowning most or all of them.

At this point, a fatal mistake was made that certainly hastened the demise of the *Birkenhead* and ended any question of whether she could be saved. Captain Salmond, hoping to free the boat from the ledge and get her floating again, ordered reverse engines. The consequence of this decision was to force the ship against the rocks and rip a hole in its bottom.

Meanwhile, those who had survived the initial flooding of the lower decks made it to the poop deck where they assembled in orderly fashion, gathered into their respective ranks, and awaited orders.

In times of crisis, it was crucial that orders be followed and that men act with speed and precision, so Lieutenant-Colonel Seton of the 74th Highlanders directed his subordinate officers to place themselves under the direct command of Captain Salmond. In return, Salmond ordered a detachment of about sixty men to the lower aft deck of the ship where they fought a losing battle to pump the flooding water out of the boat. A second detachment, equal in size to the first, was dispatched to secure the paddlebox lifeboats.

Women and Children First

About ten minutes had now passed since the initial crash and it was obvious that any prospects for salvaging the ship were slim. It was at this time that Captain Salmond would give his men their prime directive: Rescue the women and children first.

The order was obeyed. The women and children, then gathered together on the poop awning, were lifted and placed into the lifeboats. But before they were set adrift of the *Birkenhead*, the Captain ordered them to stand off, at about 150 yards from the sinking vessel.

This officer and Lieutenant Girardot of the 43rd were on watch together the night the *Birkenhead* was wrecked and heard the night orders given to the naval officer of the watch. He remained under the impression that a small grass fire high on the shore at Danger Point misled that officer who probably thought it was at the Cape Agulha lighthouse. Ensign Lucas sent home—three weeks after the wreck—an account of his experience which is of great interest. The narrative written while the circumstances were fresh in its author's memory gives us a vivid picture of the scene on that terrible night in February 1852.

Moments after the women and children had made it to apparent safety, the *Birkenhead* cracked in two pieces, with the bow section breaking off at the foremast. This caused the funnel to collapse and the lifeboat next to the port paddlebox to crash into the water and capsize. Equally disastrous for the remaining *Birkenhead* men was the fact that the largest lifeboat was rendered immoveable and useless because of the crack at the bow.

With five minutes left in the life of the *Birkenhead*, the remaining men journeyed aft and assembled orderly on the poop deck. Convinced that all was lost, Captain Salmond urged the men to swim for their lives, and even suggested that they fight to make their way to the lifeboats. At this point the two most senior officers under the command of Lieutenant Colonel Seton, Captain Wright and Lieutenant Giradot, corrected the order of Captain Salmond.

Realizing that the inadvertent effect of Captain's orders could be to give the men license to rush for the lifeboats, possibly capsizing them and injuring the women and children, Wright and Giradot commanded the men to stand fast. Not a soldier left his place. One eye-witness stated that "until the vessel disappeared there was not a cry or murmur from the soldiers or sailors."

Moments later the vessel cracked in two. This time the crack came crosswise through the engine room. That was the final blow, and with it, the stern filled with seawater. The men plunged into the water, many of them being sucked below, and the *Birkenhead* disappeared beneath the waves.

The Aftermath

After *Birkenhead* submerged, a frenzied effort ensued on the part of those sailors and soldiers still living to swim for shore or cling to the flotsam and jetsam in the waters around them. The cries of dying men went up to Heaven, as yards away women and children, in the safety of lifeboats, were forced to watch and listen. The next few hours were filled with horror as dozens of man-eating sharks began a feeding frenzy on the men floating in the water. When dawn broke, the new light revealed a sea tinged with red. Still men continued to disappear, being suddenly yanked below the water.

The blessed few who made it to the shore had to contend with the tidal current that was furious, in some cases drowning the men within yards of safety. However, in God's providence, more than one hundred and fifty appear to have survived. Not a woman or child was lost.

Birkenhead Remembered

In the years following the sinking of the *Birkenhead*, the fame of the heroic men would spread throughout the British Empire and beyond. Queen Victoria was deeply moved by the heroism of the men and caused a memorial to be erected in Chelsea Hospital in memory of the "heroic constancy and unbroken discipline" of the men. The King of Prussia, also moved by the nobility and focus of the men under intense pressure, ordered an account of the behavior of the *Birkenhead* men to be read to every regiment in his military.

Chapter 3
BIRKENHEAD VS. TITANIC

The year of the publishing of this book marks the 150th anniversary of one of the noblest acts of heroism at sea in recorded history. Yet, apart from a few small commemorative gatherings, little was said or done to remind the world about the men whose actions would popularize the expression "women and children first."

Once upon a time, every schoolboy in England and America knew the story of the H.M. Troopship *Birkenhead*. They knew, for example, that she was a symbol of all that is right and good about Christian manhood. They further knew that the troops aboard the sinking ship demonstrated to the world the meaning of discipline, duty, and charity.

But what the schoolboys of the nineteenth century did not know was that the behavior of the men aboard the *Birkenhead* would establish a maritime principle which would be embraced by another group of men during the most famous nautical disaster in history.

Comparisons between the story of the sinking of the H.M. Troopship *Birkenhead* and the R.M.S. *Titanic* are inevitable. Both ships were renowned for innovation and excellence. Both ships were captained by experienced sailors who likely took excessive risk with the boats to maintain a fast pace and minimize time at sea. Both ships had been suited with state-of-the-art watertight compartments of their day. Both ships sunk after 2:00 a.m. in the morning. In both cases, the final disaster involved a wrong decision by the leadership to reverse engines, a course of action that in the case of both boats foreclosed the possibility of survival.

However, the most notable comparison between the two tragedies is the hope offered to an entire generation because of the chivalrous behavior of the men. On both *Birkenhead* and *Titanic*, the men chose to place the lives of "women and children first," freely giving up their own lifeboat seats for the "weaker vessels" whose well being was their duty to protect.

It was not only the fact that the men of the *Birkenhead* and the *Titanic* followed the code of "women and children first" that draws inevitable comparisons, but the graciousness and deliberation with which they performed their duty.

In the case of the paddle steamer *Birkenhead*, the Highlanders and the Royal Marines faithfully assembled on deck in military formation and sank with the ship, the vast majority of them giving their lives in the process. Kipling immortalized their valor by penning the following words:

So they stood an' was still to the Birken'ead Drill, soldier an' sailor too!

Of the men assembling on the deck of the *Titanic* to bid farewell to their wives, author Wynn Craig Wade writes: "This poetic vision was the perfect balm with which to salve the newfound terror of infinite chaos that the disaster had provoked in the civilized world. The image of men standing on deck, absolutely quiet as the band played this elegiac hymn, brought tears to all who envisioned it."

The London Standard compared the behavior of the men aboard the two ships by offering the following observation:

> We are usually an undemonstrative people, but the incident of the string band of the *Titanic*, its members gathered together to play the hymn, "Nearer My God To Thee," as the great ship settled for her last plunge, left many speechless with pity. It is a great incident of history worthy to rank with the last parade on the *Birkenhead*.

One might wonder, however, had it not been for the principle of "women and children first" so faithfully followed in 1852 and then engrained in the British national psyche, would the captain of the *Titanic* have ordered and been able to sustain submission to the same principle? After all, *Titanic*'s captain, E.J. Smith, was responsible for a primarily non-military crew and a passenger roster that was more than three times larger than that of the *Birkenhead*.

Regardless, it is clear that the men of the *Birkenhead* will go down in history as the individuals who set the maritime standard for appropriate conduct to women and children in the midst of a life-threatening crisis. And for that we can all be grateful.

Chapter 4

A Survivor's Account of the Loss of the Troopship Birkenhead

The following testimony from Corporal W. Smith, who escaped death by drowning and shark attack through a blessed providence of God, is one of the more poignant of the Birkenhead *survivor accounts. Particularly touching is the fact that, though the events of February 26, 1852, seem as clear to him at the time of his writing as when they occurred fifty years prior, God had given him peace knowing that the* Birkenhead *men acted to preserve the life of women and children.*

I am an old man—old in body, if you like, but young in memory and spirit, and I can still march with some of the best of them, in spite of my seventy-five years. I can recall many things that I did in my long years of soldiering on home and foreign-service, and can picture many scenes that my eyes have witnessed.

But one event stands out with awful clearness, one memory will linger when all other impressions vanish, and I parade for the last muster—and that is, the picture of the sinking of the *Birkenhead*. From time to time the papers tell us that the only survivor of the troopship has died—that neither man nor woman nor child who was in her when she struck on Danger Point, and broke her back and sank, is left: but some of us die hard, and there is still a handful of officers and men who were hurled into a shark-infested sea in the darkness of an early morning, and heard the last hopeless cries of soldiers as the steamer disappeared. Aye, and worse than that—the wails and screams of heartbroken wives who had been torn from husbands' arms and the piteous cries of little children who were forced into the boats and rowed away, leaving to a sure and awful death those who were sacrificed that they might live.

The old King of Prussia commanded that the story of the *Birkenhead* drill and fortitude should be read to every regiment in his army; artists have painted pictures of the troops drawn up in steady ranks on deck, and poets have sung of the way the bugles rang and the drums beat; but there was no sound of bugle and no roll of drum; there was none of the stiffness of parade which pictures show—and yet there was a falling-in, a last muster, a standing shoulder to shoulder as the end came, and many a handshake and many a sobbed farewell. And how, at such a time, can even the bravest do otherwise, swept, as they were swept, from perfect peace and comfort to an unexpected doom?

Sometimes, aye, often, I wake suddenly from sleep, or start up as I smoke in my little cottage in the quiet country, and wonder whether the vision that has come again is only dreaming or reality; and I have to take my papers out and cast my mind back over the half century before I am satisfied that I have not imagined it. The whole terrible catastrophe returns as fresh and vivid now as it was then—for such a thing as that makes the same scar in your memory as an ugly wound will leave upon your body—and I know what both are.

I am in the old regiment again, the 12th Foot, which became the Suffolk when it lost its number, and I am back in the early fifties, when the British soldier's duty was to obey every order, without wondering, as they do nowadays, why it was given and whether it was right. They were the days of iron discipline and not overmuch consideration for the private soldier, who was still only a machine for fighting purposes.

There is a strong draft of us of the 12th for the Cape, where we are going out to fight the Kaffirs, and there are drafts for other regiments—Lancers, Highlanders, and Rifles amongst them.

On January 7th, 1852, we embark in the *Birkenhead* and sail for the Cape. We are in a famous ship, for the *Birkenhead* is of big size for her day, and has already made the run to the Cape in forty-five days, while other vessels in the Navy have been as long as sixty-five. Think of that, you soldiers of to day, who grumble because your steamer takes a month—but very rarely—to do the same distance.

But, after all, we are cooped up in a ship that is no bigger than many a fine ocean-going tug nowadays, She is not much more than two hundred feet long, but broad of beam and of nearly fifteen hundred tons. She has engines of 564 horsepower, and is of course driven by paddles. She has been made from a frigate into a steamer and a heavy poop and forecastle have been added to her to increase her accommodations as a troopship. Even then we are packed like sardines in a box, and have to eat and sleep and get through the time as best we can, and trouble nothing about the many little comforts we enjoy ashore.

We start at a bad time of the year, and after leaving Cork run into a lot of heavy weather that puts the crowning touch to our miseries afloat. Life and death are both with us at sea, just as they are ashore. The weary days go past and the only thing that marks one from its fellows is a birth or a death. One woman dies of consumption, and our spirits are depressed by the awful solemnity of her burial at sea. Three children are born—but at what a cost! Each mother dies—and what more striking evidence can you have of what it meant for women to sail in troopships fifty years ago?

The days pass slowly, and the *Birkenhead* steams steadily towards the south. Week follows week, and we have entered our seventh at sea when we are gladdened by the sight of Simon's Town. We reach it on February 23rd, after a voyage of forty-seven days. Now the weariness of the sea is forgotten and we are all alive with eagerness to reach the very end. Some, more lucky than the rest—how lucky they are so soon to learn—are landed, amongst them the handful of sick and more that half of the women and children. We learn definitely what we are to do, and find that the *Birkenhead* is to go at once to Port Elizabeth and East London, and that the drafts will be joining the forces of the Commander-in-Chief of South Africa, Sir Harry Smith, for service on the frontier of Cape Colony.

Who need describe the joyful expectation of those who fill the troopship? Not a man is there who does not burn to get ashore and march to the front, and there is not a soul who is not glad to think that there is only a pleasant little run along the coast before our long voyage is ended altogether. We are in perfect spirits as we steam out of Simon's Town at about five o'clock on the afternoon of February 25th.

How vividly that final run comes back again over the half century that has passed! The seas are calm and the night is clear, the daylight quickly fades and gives place to a glorious darkness. The lights are twinkling ashore, a grateful sight to us who have been so long surrounded by the tumbling seas. The stars too are shining brightly.

All is well.

From time to time as we thud bravely on from the Atlantic to the Indian Ocean we hear the sullen murmur of the surf that breaks ashore about two miles away, rising above the ever-present roar of the machinery which we no longer notice. A good look-out is kept, the leadsman is in the chains, and the watch on deck have little else to do but watch the lights glide past as the *Birkenhead* makes nearly ten miles an hour. The captain of the ship, Captain Salmond has gone below, so has the commander, and the *Birkenhead* is in charge of Mr. Davies, second master.

I go below at last and turn in, never so much as thinking of danger. I discuss the latest news with my comrades. The gossip is that Captain Salmond is pressing the ship hard for two reasons, one of which is that he wants to get ahead of the steamer Styx, which is carrying stores of war, and the other that he wishes to make a quick passage so that he can land the troops for the Commander-in-Chief, who is concentrating his forces for a grand attack upon the natives. And so that he may make his run as short as possible Captain Salmond is keeping very near the coast.

We have gone to sleep on the crowded lower deck. Midnight has passed, one o'clock comes and goes, and the ship's bell strikes again. But I do not hear the strokes of the melancholy voice that rises in the night and proclaims that all is well. I am fast asleep and unconscious.

What is that? Why this appalling shock? Why these terrible cries, this sudden panic, this staggering confusion? Why are

men crowding and struggling and all making as if by instinct for
the companion-ladder, to swarm on deck?

Why ask the question, for we know, even we who are
landsmen, that the *Birkenhead* has struck; we know that even
now some of her people are dead, drowned in their hammocks
by the rush of the sea upon them.

I do what my fellow soldiers do, what nearly every soul on
board does—struggle to the upper deck and clamor to know the
worst. There are others like me, rushing up and crowding the
deck—small space indeed for so many human beings. And it is
dark, too.

What need to ask the question which the simplest soul on
board can answer? The ship has struck on a sunken rock, and
not even her watertight compartments, of which she has no
fewer than a dozen, can save her. The *Birkenhead* with her
resistless weight driving hard has been impaled upon a cruel
submerged fang, and she is ripped just as you might rip a drum
of paper with your finger.

Panic, you ask? Confusion? Yes—both. And how can it be
otherwise when like a flash, sentence of death has been passed
upon the *Birkenhead*, and in the twinkling of an eye serenity and
safety have given place to overwhelming peril?

There are times when even the bravest of the brave
succumb to their emotions. Was not the Iron Duke himself
overcome with grief at the loss of so many of his troops at
Waterloo? No wonder, then that the men of the *Birkenhead* are
in want of steadying when the first shock of the disaster falls
upon them. Remember that most of them are very young—and
then there are the men whose wives and children are on board.
Put yourself in their places, then you will understand.

Even now, with the ship abruptly stopped, with that awful
sound of rending asunder in our ears, it seems impossible to

believe that she is doomed. How can she be, the stout vessel that has borne us so far through such troubled waters without disaster of any sort? And so near the shore, too?

I know that even now, so far as I am personally concerned, there is no suspicion that the end will be what it proves to be. I see that things are bad; I am aware that already many lives are lost; but there are the boats, the coast is very close to us, and above all things, there is the discipline—that spirit of obedience that proves stronger than the love of life itself.

I have spoken of the panic, the confusion. They have been born suddenly, but their death is just as swift. Now come the excited voices of the officers—the men who are heard in the darkness, but are not seen.

It is 'Steady, lads, steady!' and if there is a tremor in the tones—what of it? If at the first, before the drafts have found themselves, there is something of a rush for the boats, what of that, either? Does not the panic die away at the word of command? Is not the rush stopped at the very outset? Do not the men make some pitiful attempt to fall in on that sloping deck, which is already breaking under their very feet?

And why? Because there are women and children on board, and the women and children are to be saved, whatever happens to the rest.

I seem to tell the story slowly; but however fast I spoke I could not do more than talk haltingly of a thing that happened with such fatal swiftness.

Lieutenant-Colonel Seton, of the 74th Highlanders, commanding the troops on board, gathers all the officers about him, and tells them that at any cost order and discipline must be maintained. He specially charges Captain Wright of the 91st to see that Captain Salmond's instructions are obeyed, because on him alone, as a sailor, we can depend for safety.

Instantly sixty men are told off to work the chain-pumps on the lower deck, and I am one of the sixty. I go below again, and the stoutest heart might shrink from such a task. It is like descending into a dark well, for the water is already flooding the deck. But we strike out for the pumps, and in reliefs we man them and work with frantic energy. We might as well spare all our strength, because we do not make the least impression on the flood. How can we, with such a yawn in the troopship's side? She has been caught on the port side, between the foremast and the paddle-box, and the waves sweep in just like a heavy running stream.

We are up to our waists in water; but we work away at the pumps, cheering each other, saying that we shall soon be out of it and landed. But within touch of us are men drowned in their hammocks.

Officers are everywhere, steadying, encouraging, and directing. The rest of the troops are on the poop, and the women and children are there, too, drawn up in readiness to be put into one of the boats, the cutter.

Blue lights are burning, making a ghastly illumination in the darkness, and rockets crash on the stillness of the night. But no answer comes to our signals of distress. The lights are not seen, and the sound of rockets does not carry far.

What of the guns? You ask. Aye, guns would have boomed deeper, and could have been heard ashore; but we cannot fire them, because the ammunition is in the magazine, and the magazine is under water now, so that it is impossible to reach it.

Captain Salmond, like the brave commander he is, tries to repair his terrible mistake of hugging the coast too closely, and he forgets himself entirely in his wish to save his people—always the women and children first, remember. We hear his voice as he issues orders—he swings a lantern in his hand—and we know that the engines that are still workable have been turned astern.

Fatal error again! And this time final. There is more hideous grinding and tearing, and the rent in the hull is made bigger as the *Birkenhead* is backed. There is a mightier inrush of the sea and a furious hissing, as the boiler fires are drowned. But for the present we have no orders to leave our places, and we work unflaggingly at the useless pumps.

On deck they are throwing the horses overboard—the few officers' chargers that the troopship carries; and the women and the children are being driven and helped into the cutter. Can you understand what it means—that tearing away of wives and children from husbands and fathers—unhappy creatures that beg that they may die with their own loved ones rather than be saved without them?

Sixty men are at the chain-pumps; sixty more are struggling to lower the paddle-box boats. The other boats, too, are being handled

What happens? The tackle is rotten, the boats themselves are ill-found and in bad condition, so that the very means by which alone we can hope for safety are not to be relied upon in our desperate extremity. In this furious effort to get the boats away, Mr. Brodie, the master, and a number of men are lost.

There is a long swell running towards the shore and the *Birkenhead* is rolling heavily, her foremast is tottering, her funnel is threatening to collapse. It leans dangerously over towards the starboard side, and as the fight with the boats goes on the smokestack thunders down and crushes a little host of human beings on the paddle-box.

Everything now happens with paralyzing swiftness. The funnel has fallen—a great high mass of metal; the foremast has come down, and the *Birkenhead* herself has snapped in two, her fore part dropping down into deep water and her stern tilting high in the air.

Half a hundred men perish instantly at the chain-pumps, and those who do not die rush up to the deck to hear the orders given that all who can swim must jump overboard and make for the boats, which have got clear and are waiting at a safe distance so that they shall not be drawn down into the vortex.

The order is given by Captain Salmond, but other voices are heard immediately—Captain Wright's and Captain Girador's—begging that the men will stand fast, as the boats are full already with the women and children and will be swamped if the soldiers make for them.

Discipline again! And always the women and children! The men stand fast, in the very grip of certain death, and not more than two or three jump overboard and try to reach the boat, which safely gets away.

During the whole of this time, the agonies of which no man can describe, Cornet Bond, of the 12th Lancers, and Ensign Lucas, of the 73rd, have been superintending the removal of the women and children to the boat, and handing some of them to the gangway with a politeness and attention which is so wonderful that, sore as my own strait is, I cannot help smiling.

Cornet Bond, you say is still alive—now Captain R.M. Bond Shelton—and you have met and talked with him? Then he has an old *Birkenhead* soldier's best wishes for continued life as a gallant officer and gentleman! Of Ensign Lucas I can speak myself, because I lived to serve under him. Here is a letter from him, sent to me only the other month, and a box of cigars, "for all old soldiers smoke," he says.

Not twenty minutes have passed since we were sleeping peacefully and safely; now, with terrible noises, the troopship disappears, settling on the rock that has destroyed her, and with only her mainmast rising above the water.

For some minutes there is a scene that I cannot picture, there are sounds that I dare not recall; then there is something of quietness, because the sea has claimed most of these desperate bidders for existence.

Where am I now? What new terror has been added to this great tragedy of a sailor's mistake?

I am overboard and in the water, clinging to a spar, a bit of wreckage that I have reached, I know not how. I have rushed on deck in my shirt and greatcoat, just as I have been roused from sleep, and in this clothing I am adrift in the Indian Ocean, a non-swimmer, and doomed to an eighteen hour struggle in the sea to keep myself alive. I do not know that my fight will not be for so long or so terrible, or I could never see it through; but I still have faith in my salvation, and grip my spar and look about for help.

And what do I see—what do I hear?

All around me are men who have been hurled to a pitiless death, some struggling fiercely, and some clinging to any floating object from the wreck. There are awful sounds which I come to know well as the last groans or screams of men who sink to rise no more—and still more terrifying outbreaks which I do not for the moment understand, but the cause of which I quickly learn. They are the hopeless victims who are seized and killed by sharks. Remember, we are in the southern waters, in the southern summer, and the Indian Ocean thereabouts is swarming with these cruel monsters.

And yet, in all that time of suffering and terror, I am strangely undisturbed in mind. I cannot swim, but I have my spar to keep me up, and the knowledge that I am so near land is wonderfully comforting and helpful. I have a feeling too, that, having escaped so far, when so many have been swept to death, I shall be saved at last—and the conviction grows upon me even as the number of my comrades lessens.

Picture for yourself the long-drawn agony of those hours of darkness, in spite of all this, hope fills me, and the senses which are growing dulled; and imagine, if you can, the scene when the night is passing, and the tropic dawn comes quickly.

The daylight shows me dangers that the gloom has mercifully hidden. The mainmast of the sunken *Birkenhead* shoots upwards from the sea, and its spars and rigging are crowded with men, clinging, fly-like, to the ropes and timbers. With bits of mast and wood from the deck, trusses of hay, cabin furniture, and anything and everything that will float, men are holding their heads above water, casting yearning glances towards the shore which is so near and yet so far, and always looking for a sight of sail or help.

What is that strange object which is moving stealthily and swiftly through the water near me? It disappears suddenly, and I know that it is the fin of a shark, which has turned on his back for his savage and always sure attack. There is a piercing cry, and a tingeing red of the sea—and the number of survivors is lessened. Time after time that awful drama is played, and the senses are dulled until even such a death is robbed of terror.

Yet even now I cannot help wondering why some are taken and some are left by these monsters of the deep. I do know—and I am thankful for it—that they do not molest me, nor throughout my stay in the water does a shark so much as make a rush at me. They say that the sharks that night and day seized mostly those who were naked, while I had still my greatcoat on, and I keep it on for some time. But it goes at last.

The hours pass slowly, and I am parched with thirst; but I do not let the hope within me die. I am drifting to the land, inch by inch only, because I am held a prisoner in a mass of sea bamboo, which is worse than any weed, and proves the death of many a poor fellow who might otherwise escape. It is like a floating jungle. Through this enveloping obstruction I and my spar are driven by the tide towards the coast, and at last I am within a stone's throw of the land.

All this time the men, exhausted, are dropping from the mast into the sea, and are letting go their frail supports; but I am absorbed in my own position, full of my own miseries, able only to think of my own salvation. I have reached the limit of my endurance, and am the plaything only of the sullen swells that roll ashore.

And now, just when salvation seems assured, I am met by my greatest danger. I am hurled into the heavy surf, which is like to break or crush me. It is as if the ruthless sea was making one last effort to claim me, who have defied it so long, and is determined to wrench me from my spar. But I struggle desperately still, and at last, just after sundown, I am thrown, like flotsam on the beach, bruised and bleeding, hungry, thirsty, almost senseless, utterly exhausted, and stripped of every scrap of clothing—after eighteen hours in the remorseless sea.

I lie where the waves have thrown me, caring nothing, and fall into a log-like sleep till morning, when I join some of my unhappy comrades who have been saved also.

There—that is my old man's story. What else is there to tell? What else can there be?

I join my regiment, and march and fight as if there had been no *Birkenhead* disaster. It is soldiering—and it is discipline.

Yes, that all-conquering discipline—for of all the women and children not one is lost.

Because of that, and because we obeyed—I and the rest of us are satisfied.

Chapter 5
OTHER SURVIVOR ACCOUNTS

In 1902, Great Britain commemorated the fiftieth anniversary of the sinking of the *Birkenhead* with a celebration honoring the last few remaining survivors of the disaster. Originally, the celebration, initiated in Boston Linconshire, was to honor John O'Neil, a resident of Boston, believed to be the sole survivor. National attention was drawn to the event through the involvement of Field Marshal's Lord Roberts and Wolseley, both of whom lent their support to the celebration. The result was that a total of eleven survivors were discovered, each of whom were asked to provide comments about their personal role on the ship and at the time of the disaster.

The Testimony of
Cornet R.M. Bond-Selton

12TH ROYAL LANCERS, H.M.S. BIRKENHEAD

*At the time of the sinking, R.M. Bond-Selton, was Cornet Bond of the
12th Royal Lancers. After the* Birkenhead, *he continued to serve in
the military until 1858, when he retired at the rank of Captain having
served in the Cape (Kaffir War), Crimea, and the Indian Mutiny. His
testimony at the anniversary celebration included the following:*

We left Simon's Bay at seven o'clock on the evening of the
24th. At two o'clock the next morning I was awoke by the vessel
striking upon a rock. I immediately dressed myself and went on
deck, and found all in confusion. I heard the Captain give orders
to 'back her,' which I hardly think was carried into effect, as the
fires were almost immediately extinguished. He then gave
orders to Major Seton to get the horses up and throw them
overboard, and I with a sergeant and some men belonging to the
12th Lancers succeeded in doing so. I then went on the poop,
where the Captain was standing. He told me to go and get the
women and children up, which I did by carrying up two of the
latter. The others followed and were immediately lowered into
the boats. At this time the greatest order and regularity
prevailed. All the officers were then employed with gangs of
men at the pumps, and a number of soldiers, under command of
Mr. Brodie, the master, were endeavoring to haul out the paddle
box boat on the port side, which was nearly hoisted out when
the tackle broke, and it remained fixed in the air. The fore part
of the ship now broke off at the foremast, and soon after she

cracked in the middle and filled with water. A great many of the
men on the troop-deck were drowned in their hammocks, not
being able to effect an escape. All those who could succeed in
reaching the poop now crowded there, and the Captain sung
out to those that could swim 'to make for the boats,' of which
there were three, at a distance of 150 yards. They did not come
nearer for fear of being swamped. A gig on the starboard side
was then ordered to be lowered, in which Mr. Rolt, of the 12th
Lancers, who was unable to swim, and several seamen, were
seen to enter; but in lowering it one of the ropes broke, and she
was swamped. Poor Rolt rose, but was unable to reach the
shore, and was drowned. The poop immediately afterwards,
owing to the force of the water rushing up, went down, drawing
all those who were on it as well as myself under water. I rose to
the surface almost immediately. I had one of Mackintosh's life-
preservers on, which may be filled in the water, which I did.

The sea at this time was covered with struggling forms,
while the cries, piercing shrieks, and shoutings for the boats
were awful. I swam astern in hopes of being picked up by one of
them. I hailed one sixty yards off, but could not reach it as they
pulled away, I suppose for fear of too many attempting to get in.
I then turned round and made for the shore, about two miles
distant, which I finally succeeded in reaching at a little after 5
a.m. by swimming only. Two men who were swimming close to
me I saw disappear with a shriek, most probably bitten by
sharks. I fortunately hit on a landing place, but owing to the
great quantity of seaweed I had to struggle through, and being
quite exhausted, I almost failed in reaching it. I then walked up
a sort of beaten track from the beach in hopes of finding some
habitation. In doing so I perceived my horse at a short distance
standing in the water on the beach. I got him out and then
returned to the place at which I landed, when I saw a raft with

about nine men on it endeavoring to land, but they did not succeed in doing so until they saw me on the rocks standing opposite to the proper spot; they then steered straight for me, and finally landed at seven a.m. Lieutenant Girardot, of the 43rd Light Infantry, was one of them. At the same time two or three other men were thrown on the rocks off a spar, and landed very much cut and bruised and entirely naked. We all then proceeded up this track, and after two hours' march we saw a wagon up the shore, to which we went and obtained some bread and water.

The driver directed us to proceed further up the beach, and at five miles' distance we should find some fishing cottages belonging to Captain Smales, where we arrived very much fatigued at noon. Here we obtained some more bread, and then marched on to Captain Smales' residence, about twelve miles off, over the sands. On our way thither we met a bullock wagon, which took some of our men, who were too much knocked up to proceed, back to the cottages we had just left. At seven o'clock p.m. our party, consisting of two officers and four men, arrived at Captain Smales', where we were most kindly received, the men being provided with both clothes and victuals. Captain Smales immediately dispatched a messenger for the Field-Cornet and magistrate of the district, who on their arrival proceeded with us the next morning to the scene of the wreck. On our way thither we met numbers of men who had landed. Some came ashore in the paddle box boats, which had floated up; the one was full of water and the other keel uppermost. One of the ship's quartermasters told me that there were seven others in the boat with him, which was full of water. They, however, all died from cold, having been many hours in the boat and quite naked. He had his clothes on. We also met Captain Wright 91st, who had landed on the sponson: he had been along the shore and had picked up several men. Some rafts reached the shore with bodies lashed on them quite dead; other bodies washed up, some of them dreadfully mangled by sharks. Her Majesty's steamer *Rhadamanthus* hove in sight on Sunday, took us off, and brought us into Simon's Bay the next morning. The time from when the ship struck, to the period at which the poop sank and those on it were precipitated into the water, did not occupy more than twenty minutes.

After leaving the service I was with the Italian Army in 1859, when they and the French were fighting with the Austrians. In 1864 I took a bag of dispatches for the Princess of Wales to the King of Denmark. I was going to join the Danish Army, who were fighting the Prussians at Dybol. I was with the headquarters at Sonderburg. I knew the King of Denmark and the Crown Prince very well. I dined with the King twice after delivering the dispatches. Any papers I had about the *Birkenhead* were burned about four years ago, when I had the great misfortune to have my house nearly completely burned down.

The Testimony of
John Thomas Archibald

MASTERGUNNER, H.M.S. BIRKENHEAD

Thomas Archibald was the master gunner of the Birkenhead *and was washed ashore after the wreck on driftwood. He was one of the surviving Naval officers whose statements were sent home to the Board of Admiralty. This is from his account to Commodore Wyvill at Simon's Bay.*

On the morning of the 26th of February I was aroused from my bed by a severe shock. I instantly ran on deck and found the ship had struck on a rock and was rapidly sinking. I was ordered by the Captain to fire the rockets and burn the blue lights which I did. After so doing I went on the port sponson to clear away the port paddle box. We had canted the boat when the fore part of the ship went down. At the same time I and Mr. Brodie (master) were washed overboard.

When rising to the surface of the water I held on to part of the wreck. Leaving the piece of wreck I swam towards a truss of hay where I found Mr. Brodie. Finding it impossible to hold on to the hay any longer I made for part of the wreck where I found Captain Wright 91st Regiment and nine or ten men. They assisted me on the raft floating towards the shore. We picked up Mr. Barber assistant engineer and a boatswain's mate (James Lacey). We arrived on shore about one or two o'clock. Previous to landing on shore I observed a sail in the offing distant about eight miles. After landing I saw the schooner making for the wreck. We then proceeded on to Sandford's Bay at which place Captain Wright left us and procured some refreshment. Next morning proceeded to Captain Smales where we were clothed and fed until sent on board Her Majesty's steamer *Rhadamanthus.*

MEMORANDUM—In respect to the boats I saw none but the port paddle box boat, bottom up, with some seven or eight hands on her drifting towards the shore. I heard several voices calling loudly and in that strain of voice that I fancied some boat or boats very near at hand. If there had been any boat or boats present to have taken the men from the floating pieces of wreck they might with good management have been safely landed in the same cove where Captain Wright and myself were landed. They could have made several trips to and from the shore and saved a large number of men as they were some time kept upon the surface of the water by floating pieces of wreck. My opinion is that the boat that had the women and children in saved time and lives by getting the assistance of the schooner there being a great number on and about the wreck.

The Testimony of
Colour Sergeant O'Neil

Colour Sergeant John O'Neill was 75 years of age at the time of the commemoration. He survived the sinking, was wounded during the Kaffir Wars, and later served in India. The public testimonial in his honor was presented to O'Neil on May 22nd 1902 together with the following address.

SIR—We have pleasure in the name of subscribers to your Testimonial, in handing to your credit at the Stamford, Spalding and Boston Bank, the sum of £83, the amount received by us.

The kindly interest of Field Marshals Lord Roberts and Lord Wolseley in yourself and in the fund will have been very gratifying to you and the notices in the press have expressed the admiration, which we, in common with all Englishmen, feel for that historic and stirring example of the performance of duty heroically displayed at the loss of the *Birkenhead*, in which you, sir, took part, half a century ago.

We who have known you personally for years, as one of the survivors, wish to mark our sense of the privilege by offering you on your retirement, after long years of service, from the post of Drill Instructor of our Grammar School, a small earnest of our heartiest good wishes that you may enjoy many remaining years of health and happiness.

We have the honour to be, very faithfully yours,

W. WHITE, M.A., Headmaster of Boston School.
R.W. STANILAND, Lieut.-Colonel, 2nd V.B. Lincs.
Regiment.
W.H. GANE, Major Commanding 1st Position Battery,
1st Lincs. Vol. Artillery.
A.C. ADDISON, Hon. Sec.

Sgt. O'Neil said in his reply, in allusion to the cheerful obedience of orders at all times by the boys of the school:

Now small matters like this are the seeds of discipline, which is a plant of slow growth but bears fruit in due season; and as I am on the subject of discipline I might be allowed to say a word or two about the memorable disaster, the wreck of the *Birkenhead*. My share in that is soon told: simple obedience of orders, standing on deck slowly but surely sinking, whilst the women and children got safely away in the boats, then by God's providence and a long and perilous swim 'midst sharks, breakers and seaweeds, I managed to scramble ashore.

The Testimony of Lieutenant John Francis Giradot

One of the special heroes from the Birkenhead *was Liuetenant John Francis Giradot, who would later obtain the honorary rank of Lieutenant Colonel. The son of a Christian pastor, Lieutenant Giradot distinguished himself by urging the men to stay away from the lifeboats, as they were filled with women and children, and a rush on the boats could cause them to capsize. During the twenty minutes in which the boat was sinking, he stood on the stern part of the poop and successfully convinced all but two or three of the men from making an attempt on the lifeboats. Lieutenant Colonel Giradot died just months after the 1902 celebration. At the time of his death it was noted that in the years that followed the sinking of the* Birkenhead, *he went on to serve with personal valor, again saving many lives, during the Kaffir war. Several days after the disaster, on March 1, 1852, he penned a letter from Simon's Bay to his father:*

I wrote one letter to say I was safe, but for fear that it should not reach you I will send this to say I am quite well. I remained on the wreck until she went down; the suction took me down some way, and a man got hold of my leg, but I managed to kick him off and came up and struck out for some pieces of wood that were on the water and started for land, about two miles off. I was in the water about five hours, as the shore was so rocky and the surf ran so high that a great many were lost trying to land. Nearly all those that took to the water without their clothes on were taken by sharks; hundreds of them were all round us, and I saw men taken by them close to me, but as I was dressed (having on a flannel shirt and trousers) they preferred the others. I was not in the least hurt, and, am happy to say, kept my head clear; most of the officers lost their lives from losing their presence of mind and trying to take money with them, and from not throwing off their coats. There was no time to get the paddle box boats down, and a great many more might have been saved but the boats that were got down deserted us and went off. From the time she struck to when she went down was 20 minutes. When I landed I found an officer of the 12th Lancers who had swum off with a life preserver, and 14 men who had got on with bits of wood like myself. We walked up the country 11 miles to a farm belonging to Captain Smales, formerly of the 7th Dragoon Guards, who was very kind to us, and all the men that were got on shore came up to him. I hope the Government will make up our loss to us, as I have saved nothing. Metford of the 6th, the Ensign I spoke of as having his wife on board with him, went down. She, poor thing, was left here when the ship sailed for Buffalo mouth; I have just been to see her, and she looks more dead than alive, left all alone at this distance from her home, but we shall do all we can to be of service to her. God grant that we may all be spared to meet again.

The Testimony of Corporal William Smith

Corporal William Smith enlisting in the 12th Regiment of Foot at Weedon Bucks in 1848. Following the demise of the Birkenhead *he continued to serve with his regiment in the South African Bush. Over the next thirty years, he served the British Crown in numerous engagements as a member of the Mounted Rifles during the 1857 Indian Mutiny, the Colonial Wars, the Transkei War of 1877, and the Zulu war of 1877.*

After four years service in England I embarked on board the *Birkenhead* at Spithead on January 1st, 1852. We took in men and stores at Queenstown. We had it very rough in the Bay of Biscay; made Madeira; then sailed on to Sierra Leone from thence to St. Helena. At Simon's Bay we took in stores and a few Colonial troops. We left Simon's Bay about 6 p.m. on February

25th *en route* for Port Elizabeth and East London as our different corps were stationed on the frontier. We surmised that Captain Salmond R.N., commanding the vessel, was anxious to get ahead of H.M.S. *Styx* then on the Cape coast. At two o'clock in the morning on the wheel being relieved a tremendous shock was felt, and we knew the ship had struck. This was on Danger Point a short distance from Cape Agulhas. There was a panic for a short time but admirable discipline was maintained through the efforts of the officers. A few Congreve rockets were thrown up but were of no avail. A gun could not be fired as the magazine was almost instantly under water. Good order was eventually restored but the shock was so sudden. I believe twenty minutes had hardly elapsed before the vessel was in pieces. I was sleeping on the lower deck when the shock came and crowded up the ladder with others but found it difficult work. Some never came up at all but were drowned in their hammocks the water rushing in so suddenly. Most of the troops were fallen in on deck with the exception of some sixty men who were told off below to man the chain pumps; they never came up again but were all drowned like rats in a hole. After gaining the deck I went and assisted the crew in rigging the chain pumps. I remained there, and I think it was about the hardest twenty minutes work I ever did in my life. We all worked like Trojans.

As I have said there were sixty men told off. I remember nothing about reliefs. I know I remained below the whole time. I know very little about what happened on deck during this time. I think I was the only man that ever came up again from the pumps. Lieutenant Girardot was on the ladder giving orders and encouraging us. I was over my knees in water as it was gaining fast on us. I happened to be working nearest the companion ladder when one of the ship's officers told

Lieutenant Girardot that it was no use attempting to keep the water down and we had better try to get the boats out or anything in the shape of a raft. With that I sprang up the ladder on deck and not a moment too soon as immediately the main deck was under water which poured down the hatchway so that it would be impossible for any to escape. In about two minutes the main crash came and I was washed into the sea. I saw Captain Salmond on the poop deck with a lantern in his hand surrounded by a crowd. I heard him say "I will save you all and the ship too." Some short time after this the poop deck gave a lurch and went under. I don't remember his telling the men to swim out to the boats; I might have been too far off together with the noise of falling timbers. The women and children were placed in the second cutter and the horses thrown over the gangway most of them swimming ashore. A master's assistant, Mr. Richards, took charge of the boat which cleared from the sinking ship at once—had they remained the boat would have been drawn in the vortex. This and one other small boat were all that could be got afloat. Had there been time to get the long boat and the two paddle box boats afloat many more would have been saved. The boat with the women and children was fortunately sighted and picked up at sea the next day by a coasting schooner the *Lioness* and taken into Simon's Bay. A small portion of the wreck was jointed into the sunken rocks with a part of the mainmast standing, to which a few men clung for some hours, till, becoming exhausted they fell off one by one into the sea and were drowned.

I managed fortunately to meet one of the ship's spars when in the water to which I clung and getting on top I stuck tight to it as I could not swim. I was about twenty hours in the water. Some others managed to get ashore in much the same way—I should think it would be about two and a half miles. I believe most of the swimmers were drowned in miscalculating the distance as the mountains looked much nearer across the water in the darkness. Many lost their lives by the falling and smashing of timbers, others by the sharks which infested this part of the sea as the waters were tinged with blood in many places. The *Birkenhead* was an iron vessel—had she been a wooden ship she might not have broken up so quickly and there would probably have been more time and a better chance to escape. After being a long while without food we managed to scramble to a sort of farm owned by Captain Smales who had a small store. Here we got a glass of grog each and procured clothing food and shelter. Captain Wright who has served in the Cape before was the only officer who knew the coast. Information of the wreck was conveyed to the commanding officer at the Cape who forthwith dispatched the *Rhadamanthus* sloop which took us to Simon's Bay where we remained a few days to recruit our strength. We then proceeded further to join our different corps.

The Testimony of Colonel Richard Athol Nesbitt

Colonel Nesbitt was a fourteen-year-old boy traveling with his family aboard the Birkenhead *when she sank. He died in 1905 at the age of 69. He wrote the following testimony to Mr. John R. Crocker, the lighthouse keeper at Danger Point, seven months before he died.*

Yes I am one of the *Birkenhead* survivors. I was between fourteen and fifteen years old when it happened and have a very clear and distinct recollection of all that occurred. I saved myself by making for and fastening on to one of the boats to which I clung for some time after my fingers were crushed and was eventually pulled on board. We were afterwards picked up by the schooner *Lioness* and never shall I forget the great kindness of Captain and Mrs. Ramsden to all the survivors—men, women, and children. The different accounts given by some of the survivors are very correct and very interesting to me. I really cannot add in any way to its contents. Everything was carried on by great regularity and without confusion. I don't think half an hour could have elapsed from her striking until she broke up. I believe that I am the sole survivor in this Colony. I should indeed be glad to see some memorial to the wreck erected in this country; it was thanks to the assistance of the Colonists that the troops were hastening when the ship was wrecked.

The Testimony of
Corporal William Butler

12 ROYAL LANCERS, H.M.S. BIRKENHEAD

Corporal William Butler shared his testimony with Mr. W.M. Nightingale, who said of the Birkenhead *survivor that he was "as upright as a dart and as hale and hearty as possible." The testimony reads as follows.*

I was born (he says) at Shortwood Farm, one mile from Hucknall Torkard Notts, on March 19th 1830 and in 1848 joined the "Cherry Pickers" (11th Hussars), and went with them to Dublin, where volunteers were requested for the Cape of Good Hope. Five of us volunteered for the 12th Lancers, and were drafted to Cork, where we boarded the *Birkenhead*. As soon as we were out of harbour the sea was mountainous and we took fourteen days to reach Madeira. From there we went to Sierra Leone, where a stoker swam, ashore to desert. He was caught and the next morning we were all paraded to see him receive fifty lashes. Thence we went to St. Helena and from there to Simon's making 47 days. We remained at Simon's Bay a day or two, taking on board baggage, eighteen horses, hay, etc., so that the main deck was full, hay being piled nearly to the top of the funnel, leaving absolutely no room for troops to parade. We left Simon's Bay at sunset, and between twelve and one o'clock in the morning, when the sea was very calm, we ran on a reef. It was like a clap of thunder. Everyone rushed out. The Captain and officers behaved splendidly; the former sang out, 'Soldiers and sailors, keep quiet, and I will save you all" There was calm after panic; we lowered the gangway, and pitched four guns and the horses overboard. Captain Wright, of the 91st, jumped after his horse and got ashore with him. The Captain ordered Mr. Brodie, to get the paddle box boats loose. In doing so he got his thighs jammed. When the vessel went down, the boat he had loosened remained in the water keel up. I saw four men get ashore on her, one man sitting on the keel with a big coat on, the three others paddling. Three on spar also reached the shore, two men and a cabin boy; the boy sat on the spar, and the men paddled. I saw another get ashore on a truss of hay.

As to the troops being paraded it is imagination. She was loaded to the funnel. The last words I heard the Captain say were "Soldiers and sailors, I've done what I can for you. I can't do more. Those who can swim do so; those who can't climb the rigging." Then it was a rush. Two quarter boats had been lowered and the women and children put into them, all of whom were saved. These boats left the wreck at once, and remained on the water till daybreak then, seeing a vessel, they went to her, the Captain bringing her to within two miles of the wreck. She was a schooner.

The *Birkenhead* broke in two at the fore and then at the mainmast, the hind part sinking and the officers going down the mainmast, with forty odd on the mainyard, remaining above water. The schooner's boats saved all the latter; she went into Simon's Bay, where the survivors were put on board the *Castor*, about 75 in all. When the Captain told us to save ourselves, many of us jumped overboard. I had stripped, I got hold of a bit of wreckage, on which it took me about seven hours to reach the shore where the survivors mustered in lots of six to ten who knew each other and walked in the direction of Simon's Bay, taking two days to reach the same. Many, like myself, were naked. I got two gunny bags, all my covering, my head being bare, and was in the doctors' hands a month, all my hair and even skin coining off. We passed seven Dutch houses on the road, the inmates of which gave us food and seemed very much afraid of us. We remained on the *Castor* about a month, and then went in the *Rhadamanthus* to East London.

The Testimony of Mrs. Marian Parkinson

Mrs. Marian Parkinson was only a child when the Birkenhead *sank. She was traveling with her mother* en route *to see her father, Drum-Major John Robert Darkin of the Queens Regimen then serving in South Africa. On the fiftieth anniversary of the wreck, she offered the following testimony.*

I was three years and eight months old at the time of the wreck. There was only my mother and myself of our family on board the *Birkenhead*; my mother was on the way to join my father. I can remember quite well my mother taking me in her arms on deck in our night clothes and giving me to a cabin boy to hold whilst she went again down below to fetch a cloak, and they lowered me into the boat. When she got back she could not find me and all the boats had pushed off. Two officers swung mother from the side of the vessel as she was sinking and she just caught the side of the boat and fell amongst the people. If she had fallen the other way they must have left her as the boat was being drawn by the sinking vessel. We were out in the boat until one o'clock next day, a small vessel picked us up and gave us some biscuits and water and took us to Cape Town. We were not long before we started again and went up country all through the Kaffir War. I was born in the Queens and so were my brothers. My father was discharged when I was 12 years old. I was sorry when he left the Army. I liked Military life the best.

Chapter 6
THE LEGEND OF THE BIRKENHEAD TREASURE

W hat would a story about a nineteenth century shipwreck be without a tale of missing gold buried at sea? After the heroism of the men, the second greatest cause for the fame of the troopship *Birkenhead* concerns her now legendary treasure believed by many to be resting beneath the waves off Cape Danger. The legend has been fueled in part by sources within the British Archives indicating that a large cache of gold, perhaps weighing as much as three tons, was secretly stashed in the ship's powder room as part of a military pay-packet. Despite several attempts at salvaging the gold, nothing but handfuls of loose coins, believed to be among the personal effects of the passengers, has ever been recovered.

The search for the gold began as early as 1854 when a salvage team led by A.H. Adams uncovered some valuables belonging to Colonel Seton, all of which were returned to his family. No treasure boxes were recovered.

A similar salvage attempt occurred later in the nineteenth century by a team of divers under the direction of a Mr. Bandmann. In this case, the British government agreed to give two thirds of any treasure found to the salvors, while keeping the remaining portion for itself. But, alas, Mr. Bandmann's efforts were unsuccessful.

Even with the advent of modern diving technology, the *Birkenhead* treasure remained elusive. The most recent attempts on record to recover the gold occurred in 1958 and later in 1985, by Tromp van Diggelen and Dr. Allen Kayle, respectively. The latter announced in 1986 that he had identified the stern of the vessel in but 30 meters of water. Despite a fair amount of press and a lot of expense, Dr. Kayle's team salvaged a few hundred gold coins and some artifacts, but was unable to locate the principle stash containing a king's fortune in gold.

God alone knows if the sea continues to hold back the fabulous fortune of the H.M.S. *Birkenhead*, and where upon the ocean floor it lies. Perhaps it will be the next generation of adventure seekers who will discover the resting place of this golden stash. Until then, the legend of the *Birkenhead* treasure will continue to fire the imaginations of young boys and old men alike, from South Africa to the United States.

Appendix A
THE BIRKENHEAD PASSENGER LIST

NAME	RANK	UNIT	SURVIVED
Peter Allen	Private	43rd Regiment	Y
Edward Ambrose	Private	43rd Regiment	Y
George Anderson	Private	74th Highlanders	N
John Anderson	Private	43rd Light Infantry	N
D. Andrews	Private	60th Rifles	Y
A. Anthers	Private	2nd Regiment	Y
John Archbold	Gunner	Birkenhead	Y
Thomas Archer	Private	12th Regiment	N
J. Armstrong	Private	12th Regiment	N
John Ashbolt	Stoker	Birkenhead	Y
John Banden	Private	2nd Regiment	Y
Benjamin Barber	Assistant Engineer	Birkenhead	Y
Abraham Bark	Private	6th Royal Regiment	N
Barrett	Private	12th Regiment	N
Archibald Baxter	Private	74th Highlanders	N

NAME	RANK	UNIT	SURVIVED
Michael Beckett	Private	6th Royal Regiment	N
T. Bellingham	Private	12th Regiment	N
John Bennie	Private	74th Highlanders	N
James Bernard	Private	73rd Regiment	N
Henry Bewhill	Seaman	Birkenhead	Y
James Biggam	Private	73rd Regiment	N
H. Birmingham	Private	73rd Regiment	N
Joseph Birt	Private	91st Regiment	N
Robert Blackie	Private	74th Highlanders	N
Bond	Cornet	12th Lancers	Y
A.H. Booth	Lieutenant	73rd Regiment	N
W. Boswell	Private	12th Regiment	N
John Bowen	Able Seaman	Birkenhead	Y
William Boyce	Private	74th Regiment	Y
Boylan	Ensign	2nd Regiment	N
George Brackley	Private	43rd Regiment	Y
George Bradley	Private	12th Regiment	N
Daniel Brennan	Private	43rd Light Infantry	N
William Brennan	Private	73rd Regiment	N
James Brian	Private	91st Regiment	N
George Bridges	Private	12th Regiment	Y
W. Brodie	Master	Birkenhead	N
Joseph Bromley	Private	6th Royal Regiment	N
James Brookland	Private	60th Rifles	N
William Brown	Private	6th Royal Regiment	N
James Brown	Private	60th Rifles	N
Walter Bruce	Private	74th Highlanders	N
Joseph Bryan	Private	6th Royal Regiment	N
William Bryan	Private	6th Royal Regiment	N
E. Bryan	Private	73rd Regiment	N
Patrick Bryan	Private	6th Royal Regiment	N
James Buckingham	Private	91st Regiment	N
W. Buckley	Private	73rd Regiment	N
Daniel Buckley	Private	73rd Regiment	N
W. Budd	Private	2nd Regiment	Y
William Bullen	Private	43rd Light Infantry	N
D. Bunker	Private	43rd Regiment	Y
Joseph Burke	Private	2nd Regiment	N
William Burlon	Private	60th Rifles	Y

NAME	RANK	UNIT	SURVIVED
William Burton	Private	73rd Regiment	N
William Bushe	Private	73rd Regiment	Y
William Bushe	Private	6th Regiment	Y
William Butler	Sergeant	91st Regiment	N
John Butler	Private	43rd Light Infantry	N
John Byrne	Private	73rd Regiment	N
J. Byrne	Private	12th Regiment	N
John Byrne	Private	43rd Light Infantry	N
Michael Caffery	Private	73rd Regiment	N
James Callaghan	Private	60th Rifles	N
John Cantaneech	Private	74th Highlanders	N
D. Carey	Private	91st Regiment	Y
Patrick Carrigan	Private	6th Royal Regiment	N
M. Carrington	Private	12th Regiment	N
Thomas Cash	Private	73rd Regiment	Y
Dennis Caulfield	Private	6th Royal Regiment	N
James Cavanagh	Private	91st Regiment	N
Thomas Cave	Private	43rd Light Infantry	N
M. Cellars	Private	12th Regiment	N
Thomas Chadwick	Private	2nd Regiment	Y
William Chapman	Private	60th Rifles	N
Henry Cheesman	Stoker	Birkenhead	Y
William Chuse	Stoker	Birkenhead	Y
William Clark	Private	91st Regiment	N
William Clarke	Private	6th Regiment	Y
William Clay	Private	2nd Regiment	N
John Clements	Private	73rd Regiment	N
Alfred Clifford	Private	6th Royal Regiment	N
M. Clince	Private	12th Regiment	N
Coalborn	Private	12th Royal Lancers	N
G. Cocker	Private	45th Regiment	N
James Coe	Private	2nd Regiment	N
Thomas Coffin	Seaman	Birkenhead	Y
Richard Coleman	Private	2nd Regiment	N
Mathew Collins	Private	73rd Regiment	N
John Colrenshaw	Private	6th Royal Regiment	N
Thomas Con	Private	6th Regiment	Y
John Congham	Private	91st Regiment	Y
William Connel	Private	45th Regiment	N

NAME	RANK	UNIT	SURVIVED
Patrick Cooney	Private	73rd Regiment	N
John Cooper	Private	Marines	Y
John Cordie	Private	91st Regiment	Y
Charles Cornell	Private	2nd Regiment	N
John Cosgrove	Private	43rd Light Infantry	N
J. Costello	Private	12th Regiment	N
David Cousin	Private	74th Highlanders	N
Benjamin Cousins	Corporal	43rd Light Infantry	N
John Cowan	Private	74th Highlanders	N
J. Cragg	Private	12th Regiment	N
John Crocker	Private	6th Royal Regiment	N
Edward Croker	Able Seaman	Birkenhead	Y
William Culhane	Assistant Surgeon	Birkenhead	Y
H. Cull	Private	2nd Regiment	N
B. Cummings	Private	12th Regiment	N
Patrick Cunnyngham	Private	91st Regiment	Y
Francis Curtis	Corporal	60th Rifles	N
Daniel Daley	Private	91st Regiment	N
Thomas Daley	Able Seaman	Birkenhead	Y
Thomas Daniels	Private	Marines	Y
Darkins	Mrs	Civilian	Y
George Darsey	Private	73rd Regiment	N
Charles Dawson	Private	73rd Regiment	N
William Day	Private	2nd Regiment	N
William De Bank	Private	43rd Light Infantry	N
Hugh Deegan	Private	73rd Regiment	N
Deely	Assistant Engineer	Birkenhead	N
James Delayney	Private	91st Regiment	N
W. Demmack	Private	12th Regiment	N
Thomas Dews	Private	43rd Light Infantry	N
Hugh Dickson	Private	6th Royal Regiment	N
William Dobson	Private	73rd Regiment	Y
M. Dockery	Private	45th Regiment	N
John Dodd	Private	12th Lancers	Y
Robert Dolan	Private	12th Regiment	Y
William Donald	Private	74th Highlanders	N
David Donaldson	Private	74th Highlanders	N
William Donnel	Private	43rd Light Infantry	N
Henry Double	Private	2nd Regiment	Y

Name	Rank	Unit	Survived
Patrick Doyle	Private	73rd Regiment	N
John Drake	Colour Sergeant	Marines	Y
Thomas Drew	Stoker	Birkenhead	Y
Thomas Driackford	Seaman	Birkenhead	Y
James Drury	Private	91st Regiment	N
J. Dudley	Private	73rd Regiment	N
Thomas Dunn	Able Seaman	Birkenhead	Y
J. Durkin	Private	12th Regiment	N
John Dyke	Able Seaman	Birkenhead	Y
Eli Eliot	Private	60th Rifles	N
J. England	Private	12th Regiment	N
J. Englison	Private	12th Royal Lancers	N
James Evans	Private	91st Regiment	N
Hugh Feeley	Private	73rd Regiment	N
Charles Ferguson	Private	74th Regiment	Y
J. Field	Private	12th Regiment	N
R. Finn	Private	6th Royal Regiment	N
Robert Finn	Able Seaman	Birkenhead	Y
T. Fitzgerald	Private	12th Regiment	N
Mathew Fitzpatrick	Private	73rd Regiment	N
James Fitzpatrick	Private	73rd Regiment	Y
Michael Flanagan	Private	73rd Regiment	N
P. Flanagan	Private	12th Regiment	N
T. Flanley	Private	12th Regiment	N
William Fletcher	Private	6th Royal Regiment	N
Patrick Flinn	Private	91st Regiment	Y
William Flynn	Private	73rd Regiment	N
Thomas Forbes	Able Seaman	Birkenhead	Y
William Forbes	Private	2nd Regiment	N
Ford	Private	91st Regiment	N
Henry Foss	Private	60th Rifles	Y
William Frank	Private	74th Highlanders	N
O. Freeman	Private	12th Regiment	N
Michael French	Private	73rd Regiment	N
Thomas Frost	Private	60th Rifles	N
W. Fynn	Private	12th Regiment	N
Partick Gaffey	Private	91st Regiment	N
W. Gale	Boy 1st Class	Birkenhead	Y
Edward Gardner	Stoker	Birkenhead	Y

NAME	RANK	UNIT	SURVIVED
Gavin	Private	73rd Regiment	N
Michael Gavin	Private	73rd Regiment	N
Geradol	Lieutenant	43rd Foot	Y
James Gibson	Private	74th Highlanders	N
James Gildea	Private	2nd Regiment	Y
George Gilham	Private	43rd Light Infantry	N
Thomas Ginn	Private	43rd Regiment	Y
T. Gleeson	Private	2nd Regiment	Y
P. Gleeson	Private	6th Regiment	Y
James Goldin	Private	6th Regiment	Y
D.R. Goman	Private	74th Highlanders	N
Charles Gowan	Private	74th Highlanders	N
John Grady	Private	6th Royal Regiment	N
J.H. Graham	Private	74th Highlanders	N
Joseph Grant	Private	91st Regiment	N
John Grant	Private	73rd Regiment	N
R. Green	Private	73rd Regiment	Y
J. Green	Private	2nd Regiment	N
John Greenleaf	Private	2nd Regiment	N
A. Grimshaw	Private	12th Regiment	N
Gwichar	Mrs	Civilian	Y
Patrick Hagg	Private	91st Regiment	N
Stephen Haggan	Private	91st Regiment	N
John Haggart	Private	91st Regiment	Y
John Haher	Private	73rd Regiment	N
S. Hales	Private	2nd Regiment	Y
William Halfpenny	Private	73rd Regiment	Y
William H. Hall	Private	73rd Regiment	N
Arthur Hamilton	Private	60th Rifles	N
Peter Hamilton	Private	74th Highlanders	N
James Handley	Private	6th Royal Regiment	N
Thomas Handrain	Leading Stoker	Birkenhead	Y
Patrick Hanley	Private	73rd Regiment	N
J. Hanlon	Private	60th Rifles	Y
John Hannen	Private	73rd Regiment	N
C.W. Hare	Master's Assistant	Birkenhead	N
Harold	Sergeant	74th Regiment	Y
John Harper	Private	91st Regiment	N
Joseph Harris	Private	6th Royal Regiment	N

NAME	RANK	UNIT	SURVIVED
T. Harris	Boatswain	Birkenhead	N
Samuel Harris	Able Seaman	Birkenhead	Y
Thomas Harris	Able Seaman	Birkenhead	Y
Thomas Harrison	Private	74th Highlanders	N
Joseph Harrison	Corporal	43rd Light Infantry	N
Harrison	Private	43rd Regiment	Y
F. Hart	Private	12th Regiment	N
Richard Hartley	Private	74th Regiment	Y
S. Hayward	Private	12th Regiment	N
Henry Hayward	Private	91st Regiment	N
M. Healey	Private	43rd Regiment	Y
Michael Hearty	Private	12th Regiment	Y
James Henderson	Private	74th Regiment	Y
Alexander Hendry	Private	74th Highlanders	N
John Herin	Private	43rd Regiment	Y
William Hicks	Sergeant	43rd Light Infantry	N
Thomas Higgins	Private	12th Regiment	Y
G.W.S. Hire	Clerk	Birkenhead	Y
John Holden	Private	91st Regiment	Y
H. Holmes	Private	73rd Regiment	N
Michael Horhet	Private	43rd Regiment	Y
Thomas Hortly	Private	6th Regiment	Y
John Hoskins	Stoker	Birkenhead	Y
Robert Houchin	Private	73rd Regiment	N
J. Houghton	Private	43rd Light Infantry	N
John Howard	Private	2nd Regiment	N
J.R. Howard	Boy	Birkenhead	Y
Mark Hudson	Private	91st Regiment	Y
Joseph Hudson	Private	6th Royal Regiment	N
Hudson	Mrs	Civilian	Y
R. Hunt	Private	6th Regiment	Y
David Hunter	Private	74th Highlanders	N
Michael Hurley	Private	73rd Regiment	N
Patrick Hussey	Private	91st Regiment	N
G. Hutchings	Private	12th Royal Lancers	N
John Irvin	Private	12th Regiment	Y
Simon Jacobs	Private	60th Rifles	N
Henry Jacobs	Private	6th Royal Regiment	N
Thomas Jays	Private	91st Regiment	N

NAME	RANK	UNIT	SURVIVED
J. Jeffrey	Pay+Pursers Steward	Birkenhead	Y
James Johnson	Private	12th Regiment	Y
Samuel Johnston	Private	12th Regiment	N
George Justice	Private	91st Regiment	N
Henry Keane	Private	6th Royal Regiment	N
Thomas Keans	Private	Marines	Y
William Kearns	Private	73rd Regiment	N
Adam Keating	Private	45th Regiment	Y
Michael Kelcher	Private	60th Rifles	N
T. Kelcher	Private	12th Regiment	N
George Kelley	Stoker	Birkenhead	Y
J. Kelley	Private	12th Regiment	N
William Kelley	Private	60th Rifles	N
Kelley	Private	43rd Light Infantry	N
Patrick Kelly	Private	91st Regiment	N
Timothy Kelly	Private	73rd Regiment	N
M. Kelly	Private	6th Royal Regiment	N
Geroge Kemp	Private	91st Regiment	N
C. Kerrigan	Private	12th Regiment	Y
Kilberry	Sergeant	73rd Regiment	Y
John King	Stoker	Birkenhead	Y
D. Kirkford	Private	74th Regiment	Y
James Kirkwood	Private	74th Highlanders	N
John Kitchen	Private	6th Regiment	Y
William Kitching	Private	6th Royal Regiment	N
Kitchingham	Assistant Engineer	Birkenhead	N
George Knight	Private	2nd Regiment	N
John Kriffe	Private	74th Regiment	Y
James Lacey	Captain, Main Top	Birkenhead	Y
A. Lackie	Private	60th Rifles	Y
Joseph Ladd	Private	60th Rifles	N
M. Laffey	Private	60th Rifles	Y
Laing	Staff Surgeon		N
William Laird	Corporal	74th Highlanders	N
John Lamb	Private	91st Regiment	Y
C. Lambden	Private	12th Regiment	N
John Lancey	Private	91st Regiment	Y
Thomas Langan	Private	12th Regiment	Y
Thomas Langmand	Able Seaman	Birkenhead	Y

NAME	RANK	UNIT	SURVIVED
Thomas Larkin	Private	73rd Regiment	N
Patrick Lavery	Private	2nd Regiment	N
M. Lawler	Private	12th Regiment	N
George Lawrence	Private	73rd Regiment	N
E. Lee	Private	12th Regiment	N
John Lewis	Able Seaman	Birkenhead	Y
John Lewis	Private	6th Royal Regiment	N
Henry Lombrest	Private	6th Royal Regiment	N
John Lowrie	Private	74th Highlanders	N
Charles Lucas	Private	60th Rifles	N
Lucas	Lieutenant	73rd Regiment	Y
Patrick Lynch	Private	73rd Regiment	Y
George Lyons	Private	43rd Regiment	Y
Michael Maber	Private	73rd Regiment	N
Edward MacLoed	Private	74th Highlanders	N
Francis Mackenley	Private	91st Regiment	N
James Mackinnon	Private	74th Highlanders	N
James Maher	Private	60th Rifles	N
Malachi	Private	73rd Regiment	N
M. Malay	Private	2nd Regiment	Y
D. Maloney	Private	73rd Regiment	Y
Cornelius Maloney	Private	6th Royal Regiment	N
Thomas Maloney	Private	6th Royal Regiment	N
Patrick Maloney	Private	6th Royal Regiment	N
J. Maloney	Private	73rd Regiment	Y
George Marsh	Private	2nd Regiment	N
John Martin	Private	2nd Regiment	N
Henry Mather	Private	60th Rifles	Y
Charles Mathews	Boy 2nd Class	Birkenhead	Y
William Mathieson	Private	91st Regiment	N
M. Mathison	Corporal	74th Highlanders	N
Alexander Mathison	Private	74th Highlanders	N
W Matravis	Private	12th Regiment	N
Henry Maxell	Quartermaster	Birkenhead	Y
Thomas Maxwell	Private	74th Highlanders	N
Patrick May	Private	73rd Regiment	Y
John Mayn	Private	6th Royal Regiment	N
John McAcy	Private	60th Rifles	N
William McAnley	Private	74th Highlanders	N

NAME	RANK	UNIT	SURVIVED
John McCabe	Stoker	Birkenhead	Y
Patrick McCann	Private	6th Royal Regiment	N
John McCarthy	Able Seaman	Birkenhead	Y
J. McClaymont	Assistant Engineer	Birkenhead	N
P. McCrery	Private	2nd Regiment	Y
J. McDermot	Private	12th Regiment	N
John McDonald	Private	12th Regiment	Y
John McElarney	Private	74th Highlanders	N
Alex McFadden	Private	91st Regiment	N
James McGregor	Private	74th Regiment	Y
John McKee	Private	74th Regiment	Y
T. McKenzie	Private	2nd Regiment	N
McManus	Corporal	2nd Regiment	N
Allem McMay	Private	91st Regiment	Y
T. McMorrow	Private	12th Regiment	N
Thomas McMullin	Private	74th Regiment	Y
James McMurray	Private	73rd Regiment	N
John McQuade	Private	43rd Light Infantry	N
David McQuade	Private	60th Rifles	N
A. Meally	Private	12th Regiment	N
Hugh Mears	Private	6th Royal Regiment	N
William Measures	Private	91st Regiment	N
Mellins	Mrs	Civilian	Y
James Messum	Sailmaker's Mate	Birkenhead	Y
Metford	Ensign	6th Royal Regiment	N
Alexander Miller	Private	74th Highlanders	N
George Miller	Private	74th Highlanders	N
James Millham	Private	6th Royal Regiment	N
A. Mills	Private	2nd Regiment	N
A. Montgomery	Private	91st Regiment	N
Montgomery	Mrs	Civilian	Y
James Moon	Private	91st Regiment	N
Charles Mooney	Private	2nd Regiment	N
John Moore	Private	91st Regiment	N
James Moore	Private	60th Rifles	N
John Moore	Private	2nd Regiment	Y
T. Morgan	Private	12th Regiment	N
Michael Morgan	Private	6th Royal Regiment	N
R. Morrison	Private	12th Regiment	N

NAME	RANK	UNIT	SURVIVED
James Morton	Private	74th Highlanders	N
J. Mullany	Private	12th Regiment	N
Patrick Mullins	Private	91st Regiment	Y
R. Munns	Private	12th Regiment	N
D. Munro	Private	74th Regiment	Y
Alexander Murdock	Private	74th Highlanders	N
John Murphy	Private	73rd Regiment	N
Thomas Murray	Private	73rd Regiment	N
James Nasson	Private	2nd Regiment	N
A. Nathaniel	Private	74th Regiment	Y
William Neal	Carpenter's Mate	Birkenhead	Y
John Nelson	Private	74th Highlanders	N
Nesbit	Mrs	Civilian	Y
Charles Noble	Able Seaman	Birkenhead	Y
John Northoven	Private	Marines	Y
Thomas Nutall	Private	60th Rifles	Y
J. Owen	Private	12th Regiment	N
James Oxley	Private	2nd Regiment	N
Michael O'Brien	Private	73rd Regiment	Y
Patrick O'Brien	Private	60th Rifles	N
William O'Connell	Private	73rd Regiment	N
Michael O'Connell	Private	2nd Regiment	N
D. O'Connor	Private	12th Regiment	N
J. O'Davis	Second Master	Birkenhead	N
John O'Reilly	Private	73rd Regiment	Y
Robert Page	Private	2nd Regiment	Y
W. Palmer	Private	12th Regiment	N
Michael M. Parklin	Private	43rd Light Infantry	N
Thomas Peacock	Private	60th Rifles	N
Joseph Penning	Private	43rd Light Infantry	N
George Peters	Private	43rd Regiment	Y
John Peters	Private	2nd Regiment	Y
P. Peters	Private	2nd Regiment	Y
J. Pettifer	Private	12th Regiment	N
John Phalan	Able Seaman	Birkenhead	Y
David Pratt	Private	91st Regiment	N
George Price	Private	2nd Regiment	N
Thomas Pride	Private	74th Highlanders	N
Charles Prince	Private	6th Royal Regiment	N

Name	Rank	Unit	Survived
T. Purcell	Private	12th Regiment	N
Edward Quin	Private	43rd Light Infantry	N
John Quinn	Private	2nd Regiment	N
George Randall	Private	73rd Regiment	N
George Randall	Stoker	Birkenhead	Y
Charles Ranshaw	Private	43rd Light Infantry	N
John Rees	Private	60th Rifles	N
John Rennington	Private	6th Royal Regiment	N
C.R. Renwick	Assistant Engineer	Birkenhead	Y
C. Reynolds	Private	12th Regiment	N
R.B. Richards	Masters Assistant	Birkenhead	Y
John Riddlesden	Private	43rd Light Infantry	N
John Rider	Private	6th Royal Regiment	N
D. Riorden	Private	43rd Light Infantry	N
J. Roberts	Carpenter	Birkenhead	N
Robertson	Staff Asst Surgeon		N
Thomas Robertson	Private	74th Highlanders	N
W.G. Robinson	Lieutenant	73rd Regiment	N
J. Robinson	Private	91st Regiment	Y
J. Roche	Private	12th Regiment	N
Rolt	Cornet	12th Royal Lancers	N
James Rowley	Private	2nd Regiment	N
William Russel	Private	60th Rifles	N
Russel	Ensign	74th Highlanders	N
Martin Ruth	Able Seaman	Birkenhead	Y
Ebenezer Rutherfor	Private	d 74th Highlanders	N
Patrick Ryan	Private	6th Royal Regiment	N
R. Salmond	Master Commanding	Birkenhead	N
M. Schofield	Private	12th Lancers	Y
Philip Scott	Private	73rd Regiment	N
H. Scutts	Private	60th Rifles	N
William Sedgwood	Private	91st Regiment	N
Seton	Lieutenant Colonel	74th Highlanders	N
J. Sharp	Private	74th Regiment	Y
John Sharp	Private	74th Highlanders	N
William Sharp	Private	43rd Regiment	Y
G. Shaughnessy	Private	2nd Regiment	N
Duncan Shaw	Private	74th Highlanders	N
Daniel Shea	Private	73rd Regiment	N

NAME	RANK	UNIT	SURVIVED
P. Sheeham	Private	73rd Regiment	N
Timothy Sheehan	Private	43rd Light Infantry	N
R. Shepherd	Private	12th Regiment	N
Robert Shepherd	Private	73rd Regiment	N
G. Sheppard	Private	43rd Light Infantry	N
Thomas Simmons	Private	2nd Regiment	N
John Simon	Private	12th Regiment	Y
Patrick Smith	Private	91st Regiment	N
Robert Smith	Private	74th Highlanders	N
W. Smith	Private	12th Regiment	N
W.S. Smith	Private	91st Regiment	N
George Smith	Private	73rd Regiment	N
John Smith	Private	91st Regiment	N
Smith	Corporal	91st Regiment	N
William Smith	Private	12th Regiment	Y
John Smith	Private	2nd Regiment	Y
Thomas Smith	Private	60th Rifles	Y
Thomas Smith	Private	6th Royal Regiment	N
John Smith	Able Seaman	Birkenhead	Y
William Sooter	Private	60th Rifles	Y
R.D. Speer	Second Master	Birkenhead	N
Thomas Spicer	Private	6th Royal Regiment	N
W. Springs	Private	12th Regiment	N
Spruce	Mrs	Civilian	Y
J. Stanfield	Private	60th Rifles	Y
John Stanley	Private	91st Regiment	Y
Michael Starr	Private	6th Royal Regiment	N
William Steward	Private	74th Highlanders	N
Robert Steward	Private	74th Highlanders	N
Patrick Stokes	Private	60th Rifles	N
Able Stone	Ordinary Seaman	Birkenhead	Y
James Story	Private	60th Rifles	N
John Straw	Sergeant	12th Royal Lancers	N
James Sullivan	Private	73rd Regiment	N
T. Sullivan	Private	43rd Light Infantry	N
D. Sullivan	Private	73rd Regiment	Y
John Sullivan	Private	73rd Regiment	Y
Mark Summerton	Private	6th Royal Regiment	N
John Sweeny	Private	91st Regiment	N

NAME	RANK	UNIT	SURVIVED
James Tarney	Private	91st Regiment	N
Patrick Taylor	Private	73rd Regiment	Y
George Taylor	Private	74th Regiment	Y
Terbe	Sergeant	6th Regiment	Y
Nathaniel Thomas	Private	2nd Regiment	N
Adam Thompson	Private	74th Highlanders	N
J. Thompson	Private	12th Regiment	N
John Thompson	Private	74th Highlanders	N
James Thompson	Private	60th Rifles	N
John Tierney	Private	6th Royal Regiment	N
R. Tiggle	Able Seaman	Birkenhead	Y
W. Tigne	Private	12th Regiment	N
George Till	Able Seaman	Birkenhead	Y
Michael Tonen	Private	73rd Regiment	N
Edward Torpy	Private	6th Royal Regiment	N
William Tuck	Private	Marines	Y
H. Tucker	Private	43rd Light Infantry	N
George Tully	Private	6th Royal Regiment	N
Benjamin Turner	Boy 1st Class	Birkenhead	Y
Francis Turner	Private	74th Highlanders	N
Henry Vernon	Private	2nd Regiment	Y
Samuel Vesse	Private	2nd Regiment	N
Vickery	Private	43rd Light Infantry	N
James Wade	Private	6th Regiment	Y
T. Wales	Private	12th Regiment	N
J. Walker	Private	2nd Regiment	N
Robert Walker	Private	74th Highlanders	N
G. Walker	Private	12th Regiment	Y
John Wallis	Private	60th Rifles	N
T. Walsh	Private	91st Regiment	N
E. Walshe	Private	6th Regiment	Y
John Wamsley	Private	91st Regiment	Y
P. Ward	Private	12th Regiment	Y
Daniel Waters	Private	12th Regiment	Y
George Watson	Private	74th Highlanders	N
B. Webster	Private	2nd Regiment	N
Maurice Welch	Private	43rd Light Infantry	N
William Welch	Private	6th Regiment	Y
George Weller	Private	2nd Regiment	N

Name	Rank	Unit	Survived
George Wells	Private	12th Regiment	Y
C. Wells	Private	73rd Regiment	N
J. West	Private	6th Royal Regiment	N
James West	Private	43rd Regiment	Y
W.H. Wheeler	Private	2nd Regiment	N
Andrew White	Mr	Civilian	N
Thomas White	Private	6th Royal Regiment	N
G. White	Private	2nd Regiment	Y
W Whyham	Chief Engineer	Birkenhead	N
William Wilkins	Private	60th Rifles	N
William Wilkinson	Private	60th Rifles	N
W. Wilson	Private	12th Regiment	N
James Wilson	Private	60th Rifles	N
James Wilson	Private	73rd Regiment	N
Edward Wilson	Boatswain's Mate	Birkenhead	Y
George Windon	Able Seaman	Birkenhead	Y
Alex Winnington	Private	91st Regiment	N
Fred Winterbottom	Private	91st Regiment	Y
William Wood	Private	73rd Regiment	Y
John Wood	Stoker	Birkenhead	Y
William Woodman	Private	91st Regiment	N
William Woodward	Seaman	Birkenhead	Y
James Woodward	Private	43rd Regiment	Y
Thomas Woolfall	Private	2nd Regiment	N
William Woolward	Private	60th Rifles	N
J. Wootton	Private	12th Regiment	N
Benjamin Worill	Private	2nd Regiment	Y
George Worth	Private	6th Royal Regiment	N
Wright	Captain	91st Regiment	Y
William Wybrow	Private	91st Regiment	N
Christopher Wyer	Private	91st Regiment	N
George Wyndham	Boy 1st Class	Birkenhead	Y
John Yule	Private	12th Regiment	Y
(Bandsman) Zwyker	Private	2nd Regiment	N

Appendix B
SOLDIER AND SAILOR TOO
(THE ROYAL REGIMENT OF MARINES)

As I was spittin' into the Ditch aboard o' the *Crocodile*,
I seed a man on a man-o'-war got up in the Reg'lars' style.
'E was scrapin' the paint from off of 'er plates, an' I sez to 'im,
   "Oo are you?"
Sez 'e, "I'm a Jolly—'Er Majesty's Jolly—soldier an' sailor too!"
Now 'is work begins by [who] knows when, and 'is work is
   never through;
'E isn't one of the reg'lar Line, nor 'e isn't one of the crew.
'E's a kind of a giddy harumfrodite—soldier an' sailor too!

An', after I met 'im all over the world, a-doin' all kinds of things,
Like landin' 'isself with a Gatlin' gun to talk to them 'eathen
   kings;
'E sleeps in an 'ammick instead of a cot, an' 'e drills with
   the deck on a slew,
'An 'e sweats like a Jolly—'Er Majesty's Jolly—soldier an'
   sailor too!

For there isn't a job on the top o' the earth the beggar don't
      know, nor do—
You can leave 'im at night on a bald man's 'ead, to paddle
      'is own canoe—
'E's a sort of a bloomin' cosmopolouse—soldier an' sailor too.

We've fought 'em in trooper, we've fought 'em in dock, and
      [talked] with 'em in betweens,
      When they called us the seasick scull'ry-maids, an we
      called 'em the [Cras-]Marines;
But, when we was down for a double fatigue, from Woolwich
      to Bernardmyo,
We sent for the Jollies—'Er Majesty's Jollies—soldier an'
      sailor too!
They think for 'emselves, an' they [take] for 'emselves, 'an
      they never ask what's to do,
But they're camped an' fed an' they're up an' fed before our
      bugle's blew.
Ho! they ain't no limpin' procrastitutes—soldier an' sailor too.

You may say we are fond of an 'arness-cut, or 'ootin in
      barrack-yards,
Or startin' a Board School mutiny along o' the Onion Guards;
But once in a while we can finish in style for the ends of the
      earth to view,
The same as the Jollies—'Er Majesty's Jollies—soldier an'
      sailor too!
They come of our lot, they was brothers to us; they was
      beggars we'd met an' knew;
Yes, barrin' an inch in the chest an' the arm, they was doubles
      o' me an' you;
For they weren't no special chrysanthemums—soldier an'
      sailor too!

To take your chance in the thick of a rush with firing all about,
Is nothing so bad when you've cover to 'and, 'an leave an'
    likin' to shout;
But to stand an' be still to the *Birken'ead* Drill is a [rough]
    tough bullet to chew.
An' they done it, the Jollies—'Er Majesty's Jollies—soldier an'
    sailor too!
Their work was done when it 'adn't begun; they was younger
    nor me an' you;
Their choice it was plain between drownin' in 'eaps an' bein'
    mopped by the screw,
So they stood an' was still to the *Birken'ead* Drill, soldier an'
    sailor too!

We're most of us liars, we're 'arf of us thieves 'an the rest are
    as rank as can be,
But once in a while we can finish in style (which I 'ope it won't
    'appen to me).
But it makes you think better 'o you an' your friends, an' the
    work you may 'ave to do,
When you think o' the sinkin' *Victorier*'s Jollies—soldiers an'
    sailor too!
Now there isn't no room for to say ye don't know—they 'ave
    proved it plain 'an true—
That whether it's Widow, or whether it's ship, *Victorier*'s work
    is to do,
An' they done it, the Jollies—'Er Majesty's Jollies—soldier an'
    sailor too!

RUDYARD KIPLING